DADGAD
Ragtime and Early Jazz

by
Rob MacKillop

Online Audio   www.melbay.com/30568MEB

Contents

INTRODUCTION

Welcome to *DADGAD Ragtime and Early Jazz*!

This book marks the fifth in my series of DADGAD books published by Mel Bay. While the other books have been of the easy to intermediate levels, this book demands at times a fairly advanced technique, so I would call it intermediate to advanced. But just keep in mind the words of the great Scott Joplin:

**"Play slowly until you catch the swing,
and never play ragtime fast at any time."**

**"Do not play this piece fast.
It is never right to play Ragtime fast."**

So, if you are finding the fingering a little demanding in certain places, take your time, slow down, there is no hurry.

I've chosen a few of my favourite rags that I once arranged for the Scottish Early Ragtime Orchestra, consisting of mainly banjos, with clarinet and cello. Scott Joplin appears, naturally, but also James Scott, Charles L. Johnson, Herman Roland, and the banjo player extraordinaire, Fred Van Eps.

I've also included early jazz pieces from the late teens, early twenties, by A. J. Weidt, who originally wrote rag- and pop-style pieces for 5-string banjo, before embracing the new "jazzier" tenor banjo. It's interesting to see how "ragging" a melody gave way to "jazzing."

The, admittedly, odd fellow in the pack is Blind Boy Fuller, who played guitar in the Piedmont style. I wrote an arrangement of the accompaniment to his, "Meat Shakin' Woman", augmenting it with a B section of my own invention. The fingerpicking style is not a million miles away from the rest of the book, though it has a voice of its own as well.

Well, there you have it. Five books in DADGAD tuning, from easy to advanced, covering different styles: Celtic, Blues, Classical, Old Time and Bluegrass, Ragtime and Early Jazz. I hope you enjoy working through them. Let me know your thoughts at http://RobMacKillop.net/DADGAD where Skype tuition is also available.

Rob MacKillop
Edinburgh
January 2017

Notes on the Tunes

A Rag-Time Episode by Paul Eno
YouTube video: https://youtu.be/x7H9X4cNPSI
This is a fun piece to play. Paul Eno (1869 - 1924), a ragtime orchestra leader from Philadelphia, wrote many great ragtime pieces for band and also solo banjo. A few of the latter were recorded by Fred Van Eps, Olly Oakley, and Vess Osman, among others. Note the form of the song and the order in which different sections appear. I've tried to be clear on the written page, but any doubts will be cleared up by listening to the accompanying recordings to this edition.

Blue Stocking by A. J. Weidt
YouTube video: https://youtu.be/XvliMAct-kl
From 1921, this is a fine example of an early jazz influence on a rag and popular music composer, Albert J. Weidt (1866 - 1945). He was a prolific composer for guitar (over 90 published pieces) and director of various mandolin and guitar orchestras based in Newark, New Jersey.

Calliope Rag by James Scott
YouTube video: https://youtu.be/OrQt4DhQe-w (14 minutes in)
The first of two pieces by James Scott (1885 - 1938), son of former slaves from Missouri. Scott Joplin helped James Scott's career by introducing him to his own publisher. "Calliope" here refers to the steam-driven organs of the showboats on the Mississippi.

Dill Pickles Rag by Charles L. Johnson
"Dill Pickles" sold over a million copies when first released, helping to sustain the career of Charles L. Johnson (1876 - 1950). He was born in Kansas City, Kansas, neatly rounding out his life in Kansas City, Missouri. He published over 300 works, but only 40 rags. Despite that, he has some renown as a great ragtime composer.

Grace and Beauty by James Scott
YouTube video: https://youtu.be/jbwhOklgsbA (7'50" in)
Arguably Scott's finest work, full of grace and beauty, for sure. The final section always struck me as a little unusual. It turns out to be in the style of a "Ring Shout", a form of a circular, shuffling dance of praise, performed by African slaves. A fascinating piece of music.

Homage to Blind Boy Fuller by Fuller/MacKillop

Born in North Carolina Fulton Allen (c.1904 - 1941), or Blind Boy Fuller as he became known, grew to be one of the most popular Piedmont stylists between the two World Wars. Piedmont players used the right-hand thumb on alternating bass strings, while picking syncopated melodies with a ragtime influence on the upper strings. I've adapted the accompaniment to one of his more amusing songs, "Meat Shakin' Woman" for the A section. The B section is my own. And together they form a homage to this great guitar picker.

My Lady Jazz by A. J. Weidt

YouTube video: https://youtu.be/lj4QdlTRsfM

Another Weidt piece from the early popular jazz period, published in 1921. Play slow until you get that swing, then speed it up a little, but not so much it gets uncomfortable to play. Above all, have fun with it.

Rag Pickings by Fred Van Eps

Excellent biography of Fred Van Eps here:

http://ragpiano.com/perform/fvaneps.shtml

YouTube video: https://youtu.be/MmpxGKA-e-A

Fred Van Eps (1878 - 1960) was one of the greatest five-string banjo players of all time; he even played guitar with Benny Goodman and others when the banjo became less popular. His early ragtime recordings are well worth seeking out.

Sun Flower Slow Drag by Scott Joplin and Scott Hayden

YouTube video: https://youtu.be/OrQt4DhQe-w (2 minutes in)

A beautiful piece by Scott Joplin (1868 - 1917) and Scott Hayden (1882 - 1915). Joplin included a slow drag in his opera, *Treemonisha*, with the following instructions:

1. The slow drag must begin on the first beat of each measure.
2. When moving forward, drag the left foot; when moving backward, drag the right foot.
3. When moving sideways to the right, drag the left foot; when moving sideways to the left, drag the right foot.
4. When prancing, your steps must come on each beat of the measure.
5. When marching, and when sliding, your steps must come on the first and third beat of each measure.
6. Hop and skip on second beat of measure. Double the Schottische step to fit the slow music.

Sunflower Dance by Herman Rowland
YouTube video: https://youtu.be/5dWJZBMtD5U
Ear-worm alert! Once heard, you'll be singing this one all day long. It was very popular in the 1880s, and audiences still love it today. It has an alternative title of, "With the Tide - Schottische."

The Entertainer by Scott Joplin
YouTube video: https://youtu.be/6496nf1itrg
A classic rag, though possibly more popular since the 1970s than when first published in 1902. It was ranked number 10 in the Recording Industry Association of America's "Songs of the Century". Its composer, Scott Joplin (1867/8 - 1917) was in his own lifetime hailed as the greatest ragtime composer, and history has not changed that opinion.

Weeping Willow by Scott Joplin
YouTube video - piano roll: https://youtu.be/4QNimiMBVO8
A less popular, but no less beautiful rag from Joplin, "Weeping Willow" creates some tricky moments in any tuning for guitarists, but the effort is well worth it. The A section melody is sublime, and the rest of the work contains many interesting moments. Once firmly under your fingers, I'm sure you'll love playing this classic rag.

A Rag-Time Episode

Form: AABBCBDDBcoda

Arranged by
Rob MacKillop

Paul Eno

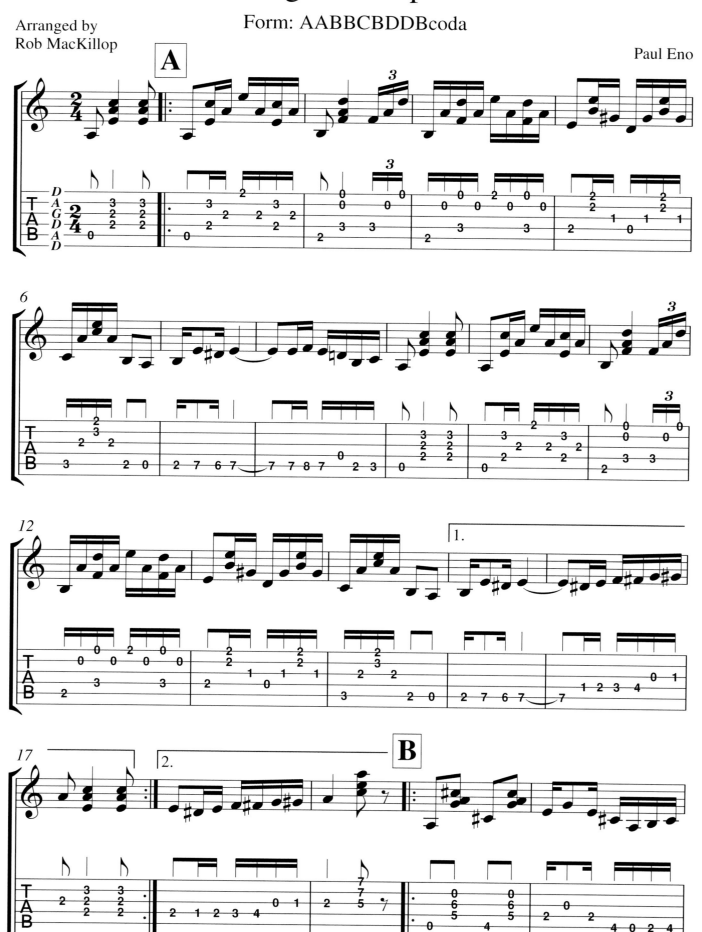

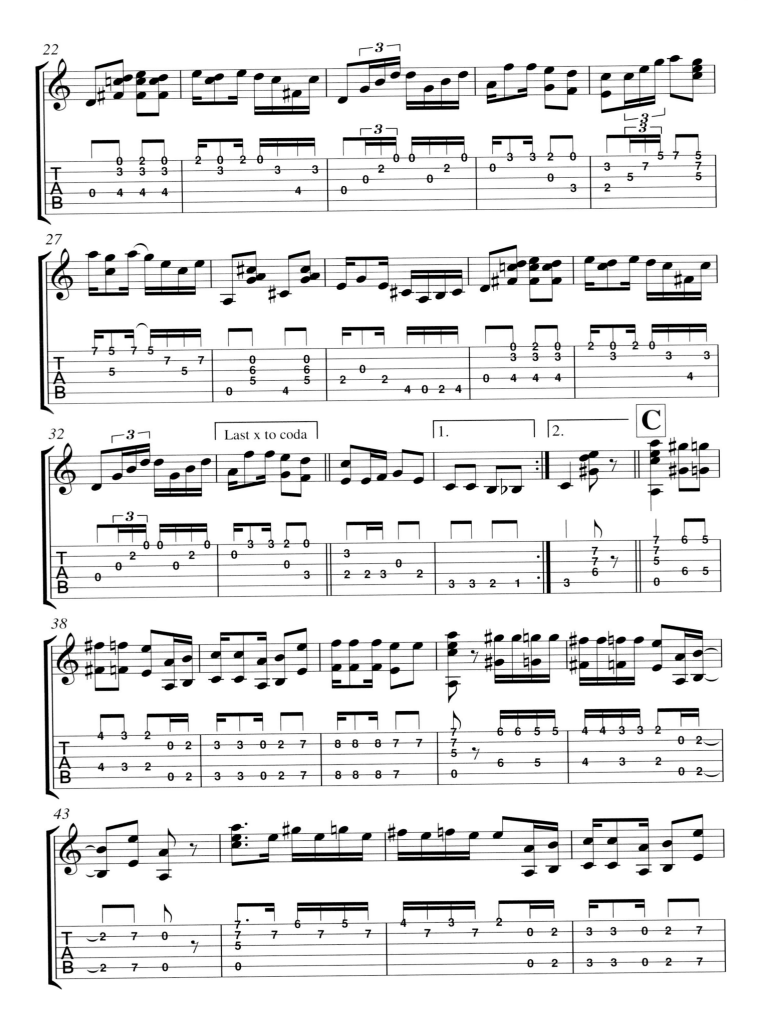

Last x to coda

8

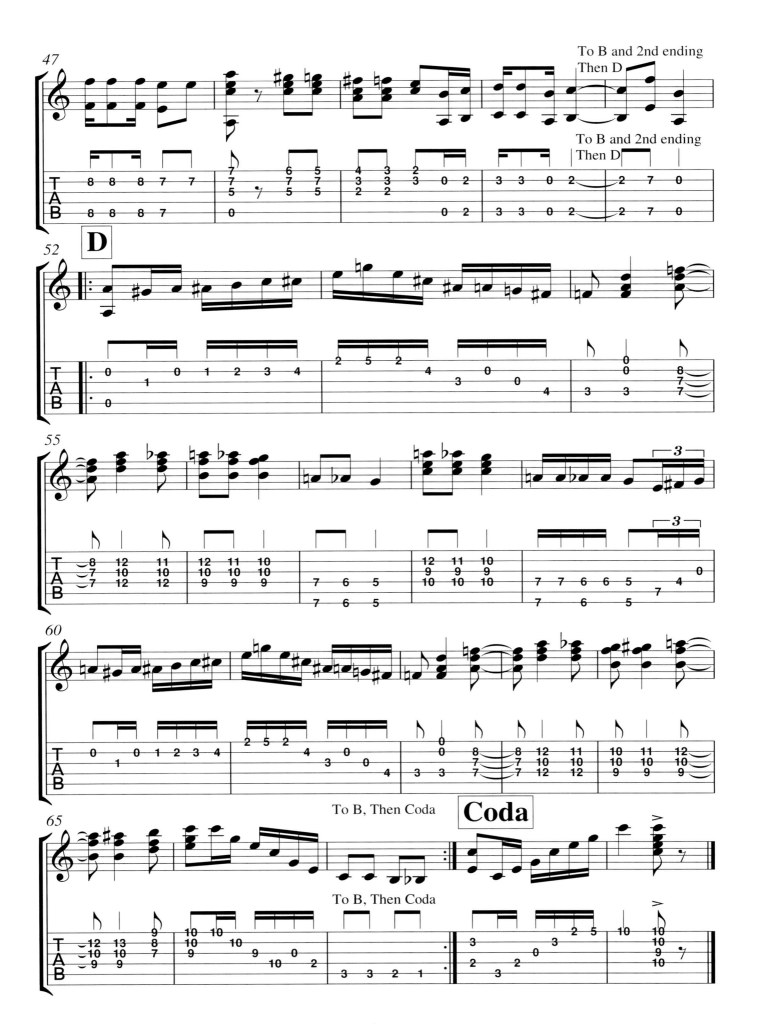

Blue Stocking
Form: ABBCBDDAB

Arr. Rob MacKillop

A.J.Weidt

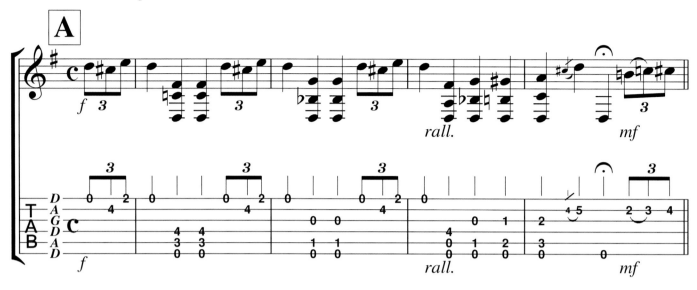

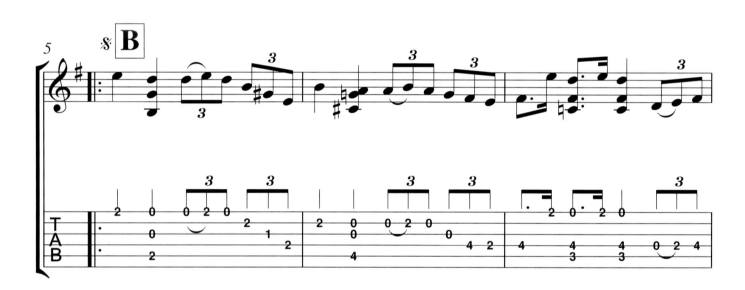

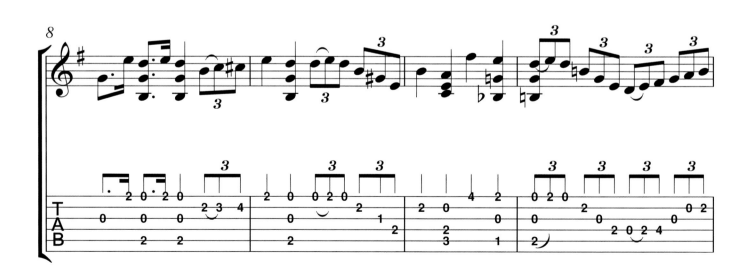

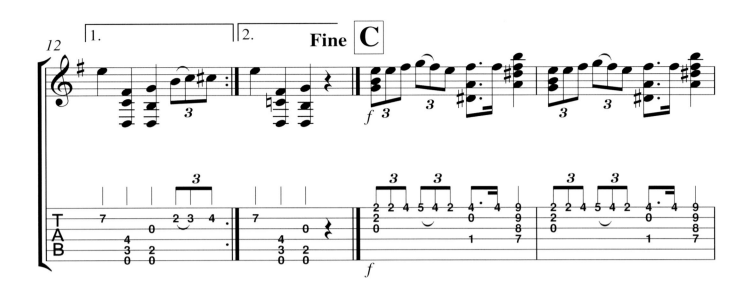

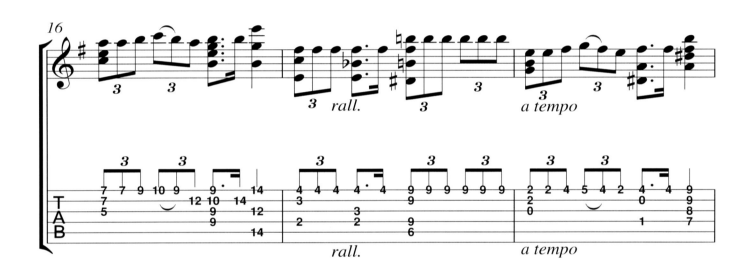

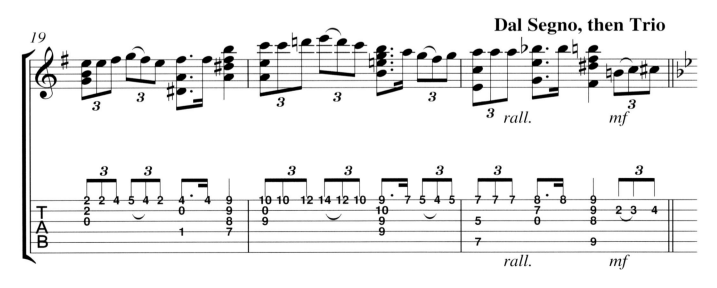

11

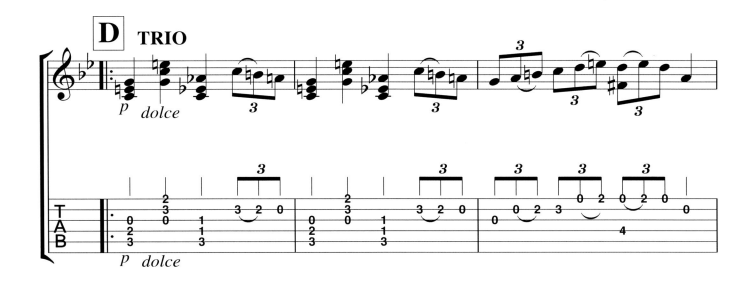

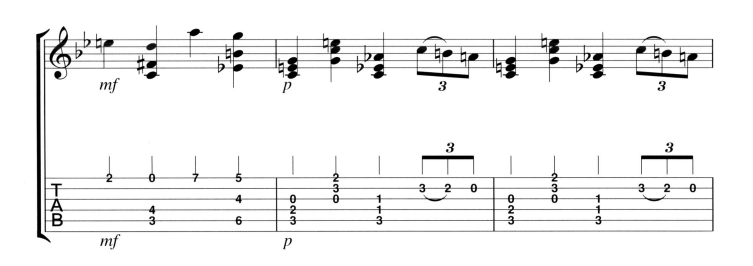

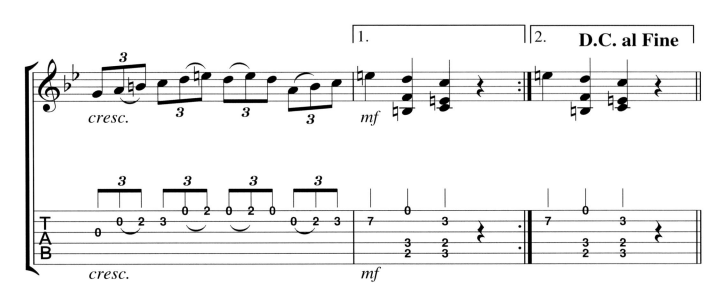

Calliope Rag
Form: IntroAABBADDA

Arr. Rob MacKillop

James Scott

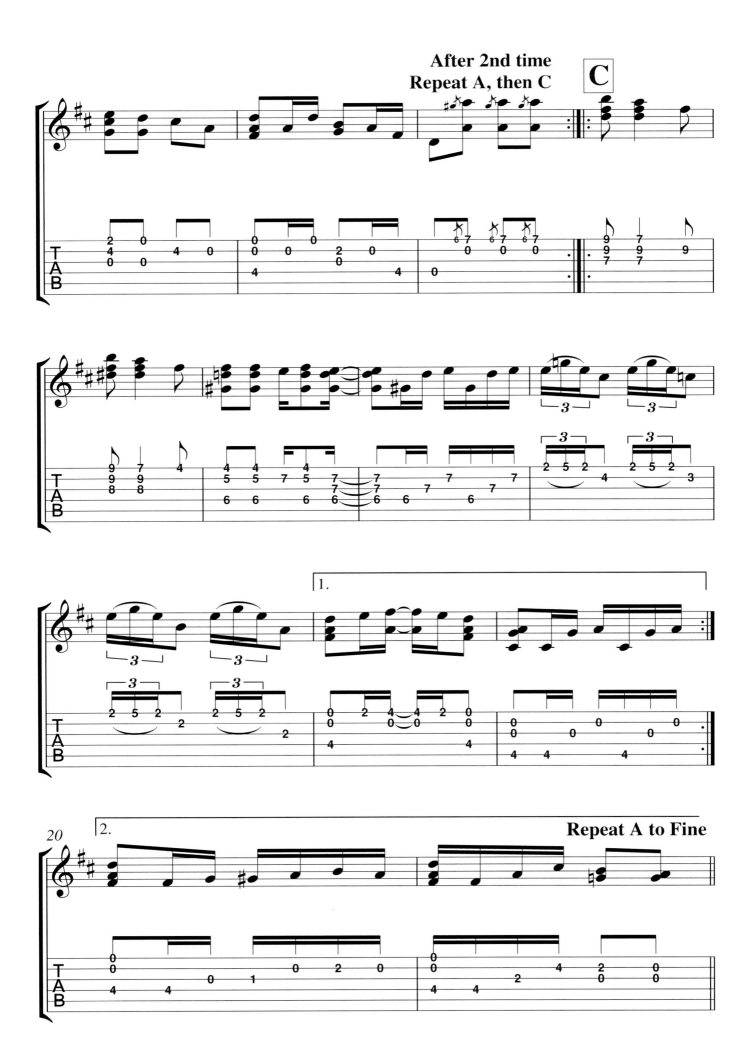

Dill Pickles Rag

Arr. Rob MacKillop

Charles L. Johnson, 1906

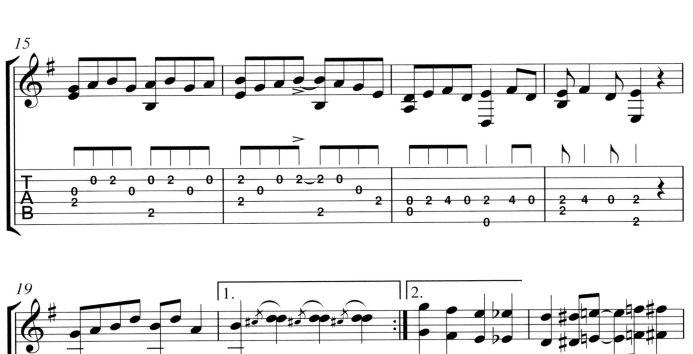

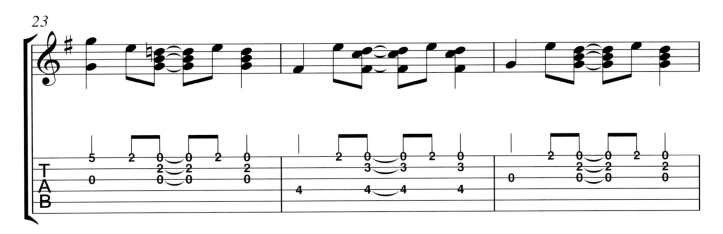

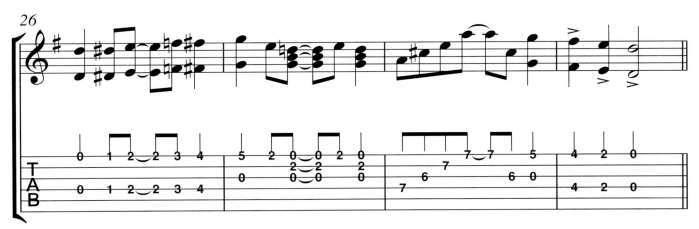

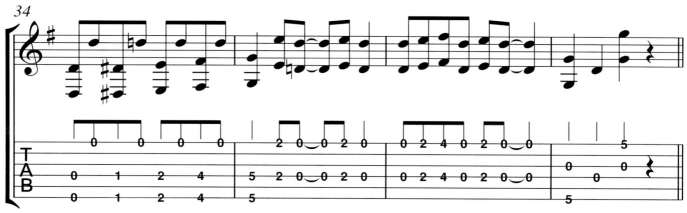

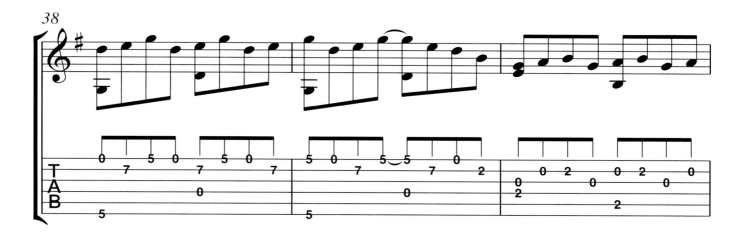

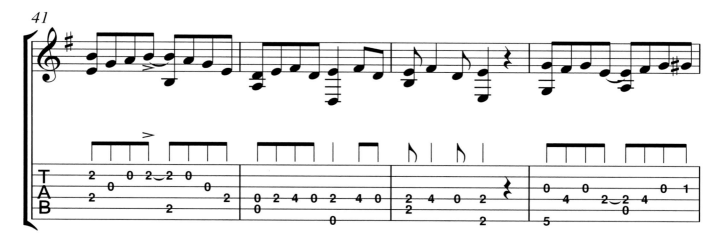

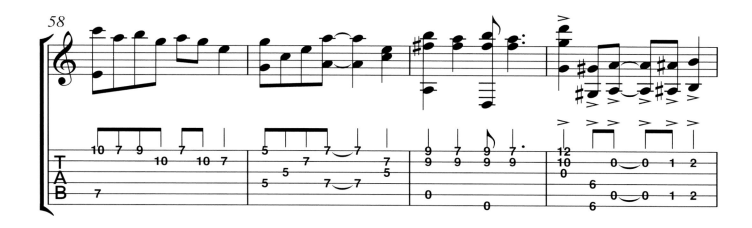

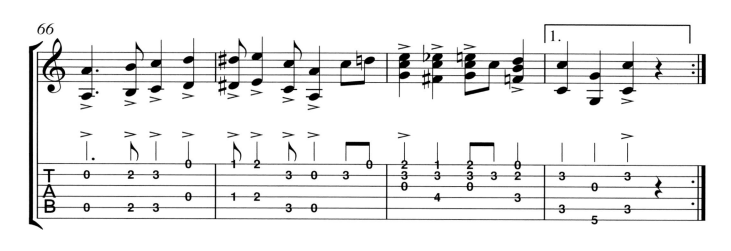

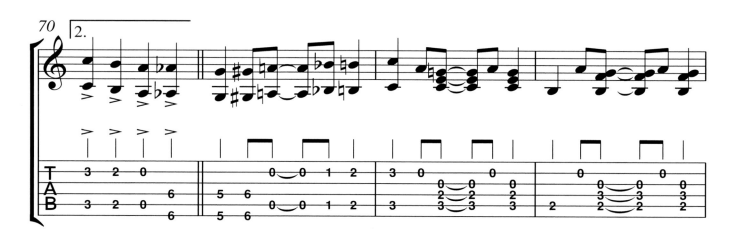

21

Grace and Beauty

IntroAABBAInterludeCCDD

Arr. Rob MacKillop

James Scott, 1910

Intro:

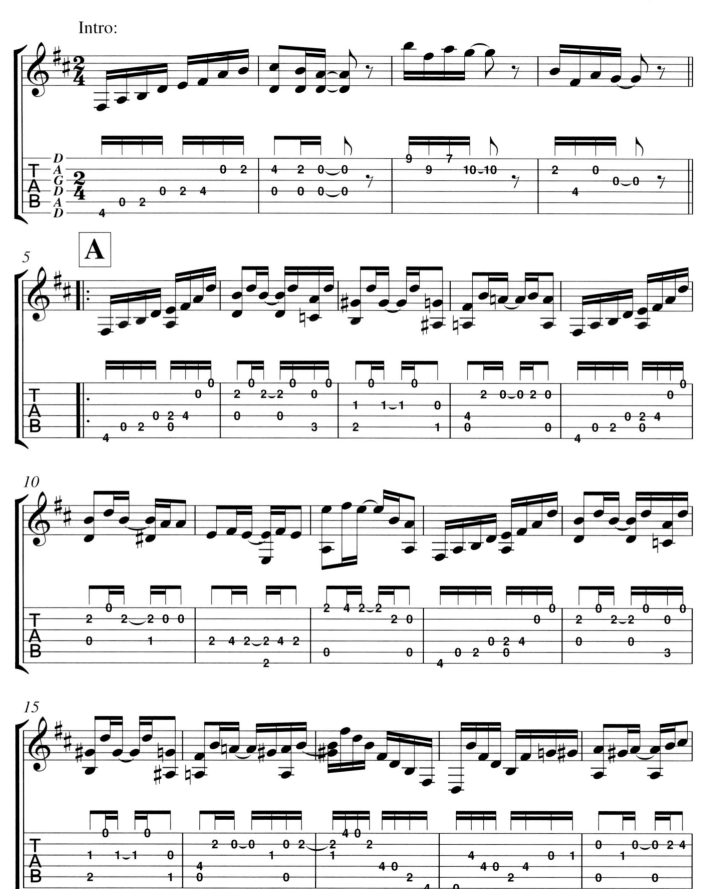

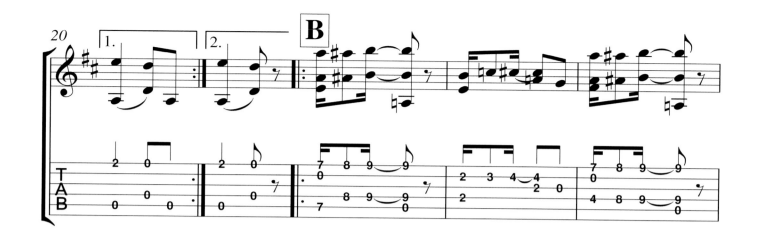

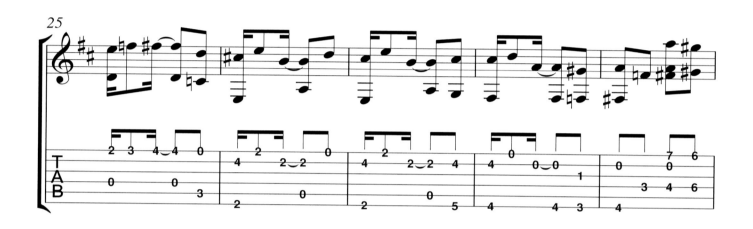

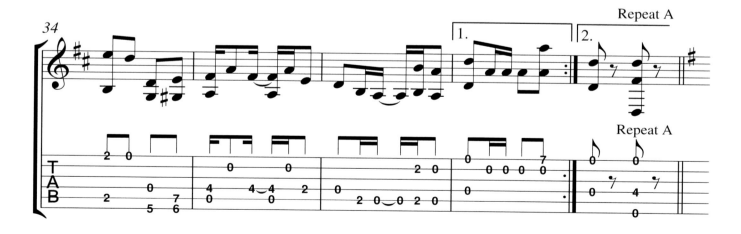

Interlude

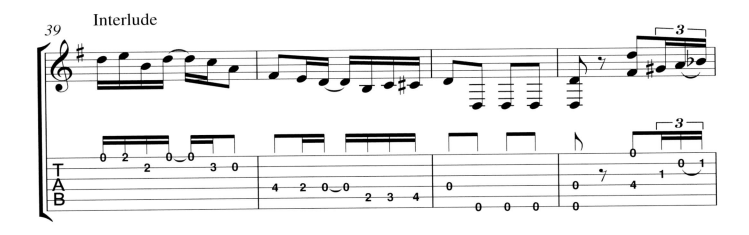

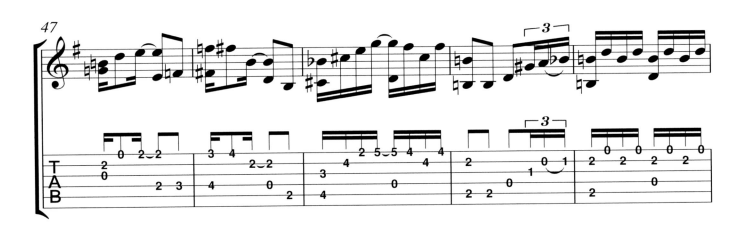

Homage to Blind Boy Fuller

Form: AABBAcoda

Arr. Rob MacKillop

Fuller/MacKillop

3rd time to Coda

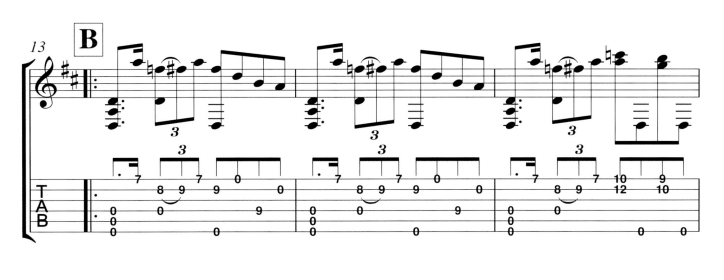

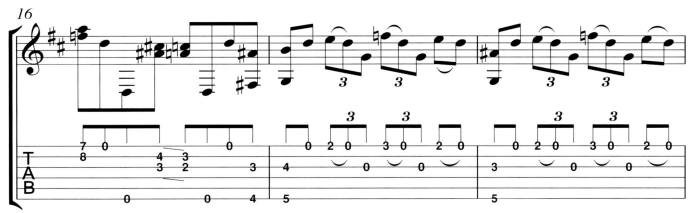

Coda

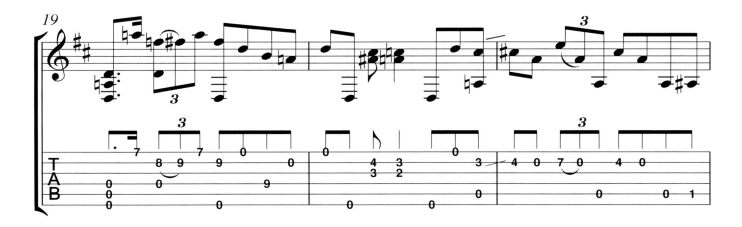

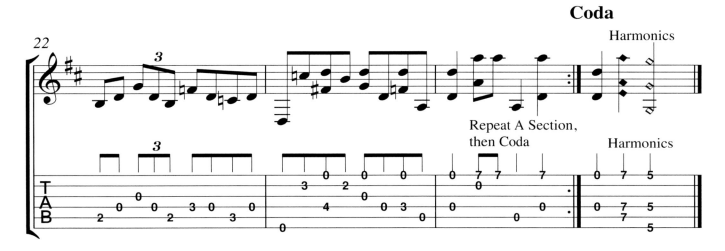

My Lady Jazz

Arr. Rob MacKillop

A.J.Weidt

Intro:

28

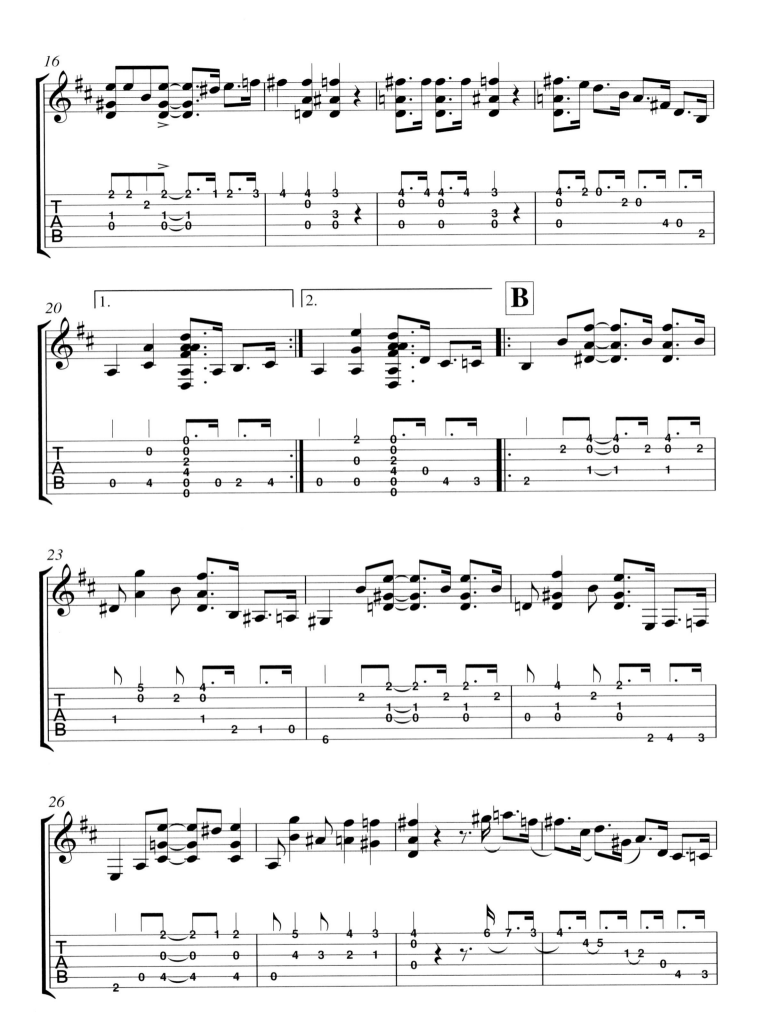

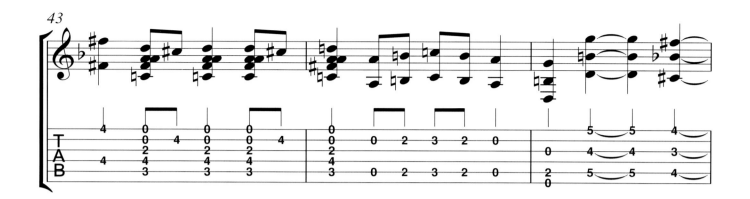

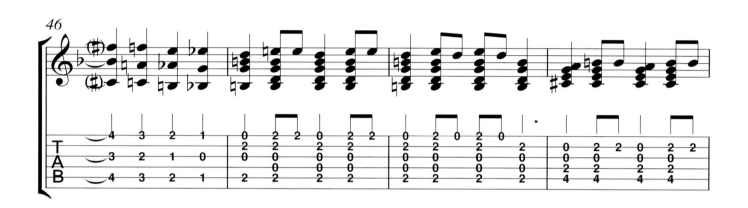

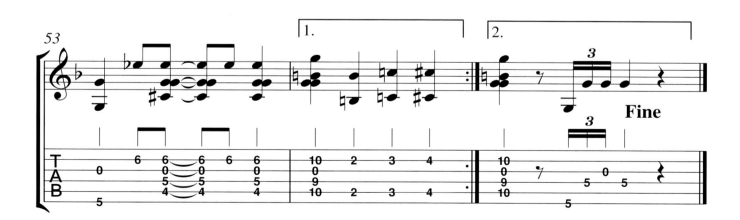

Rag Pickings

Arr. Rob MacKillop

Fred Van Eps

Intro:

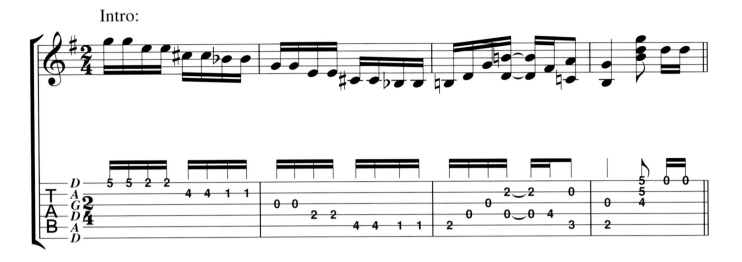

A

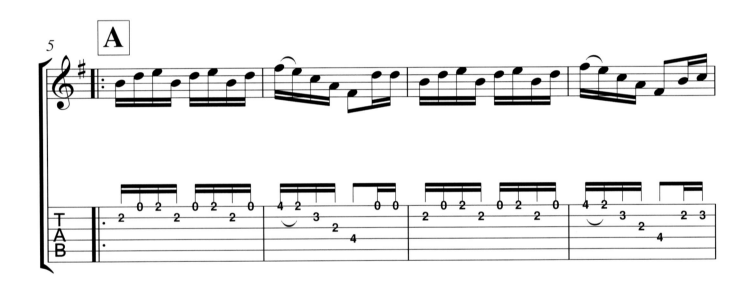

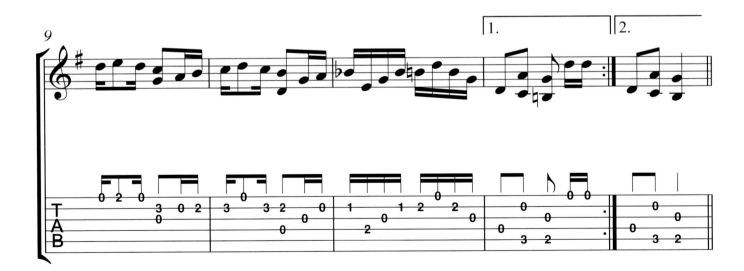

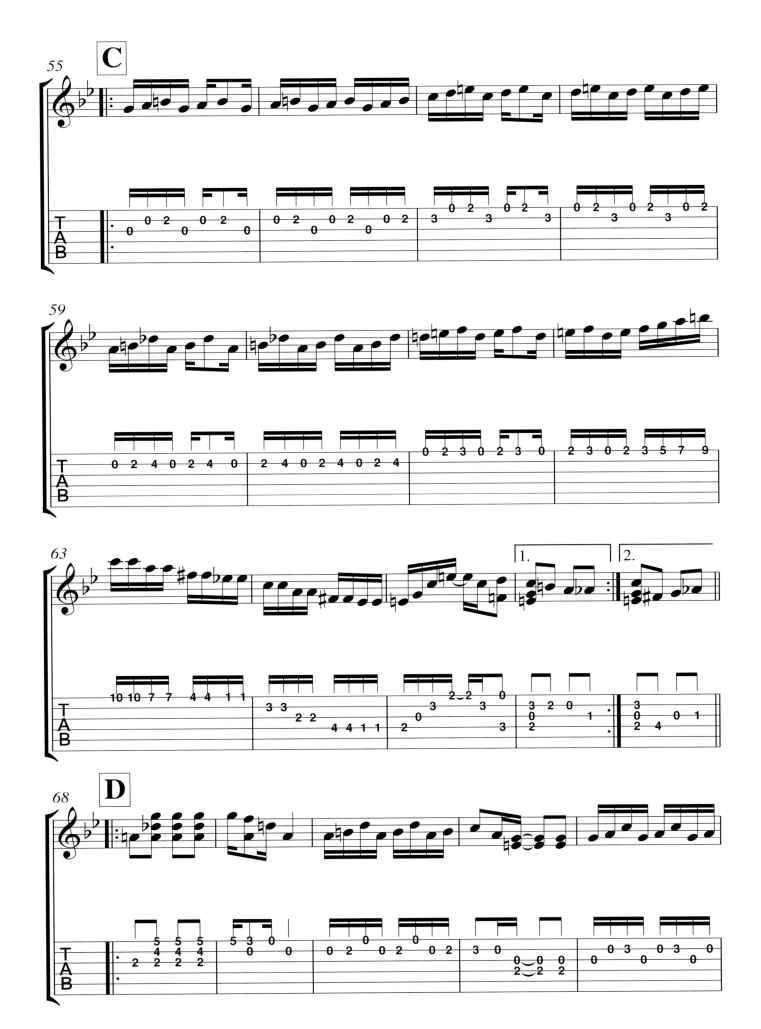

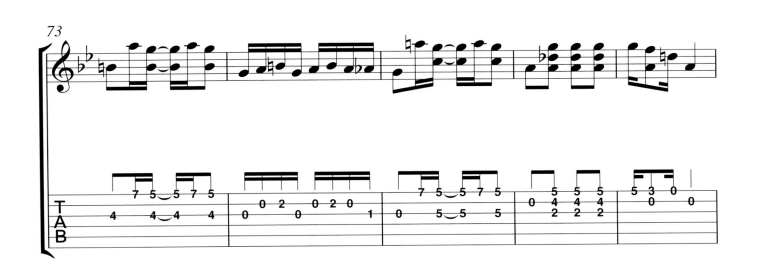

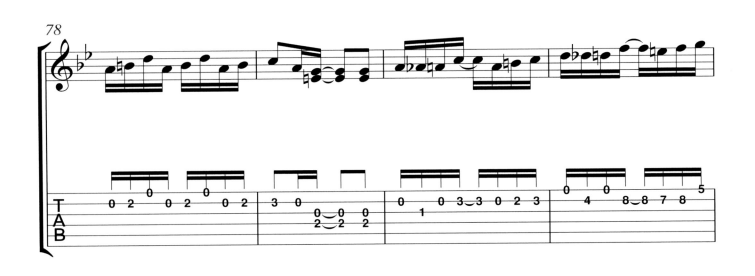

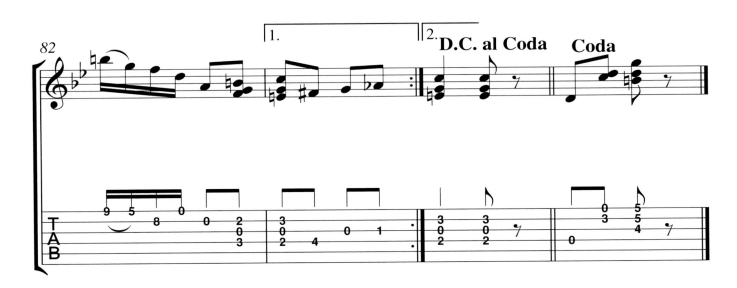

Sun Flower Slow Drag
Form: IntroAABBACCDD

Scott Joplin
and
Scott Hayden

Arr. Rob MacKillop

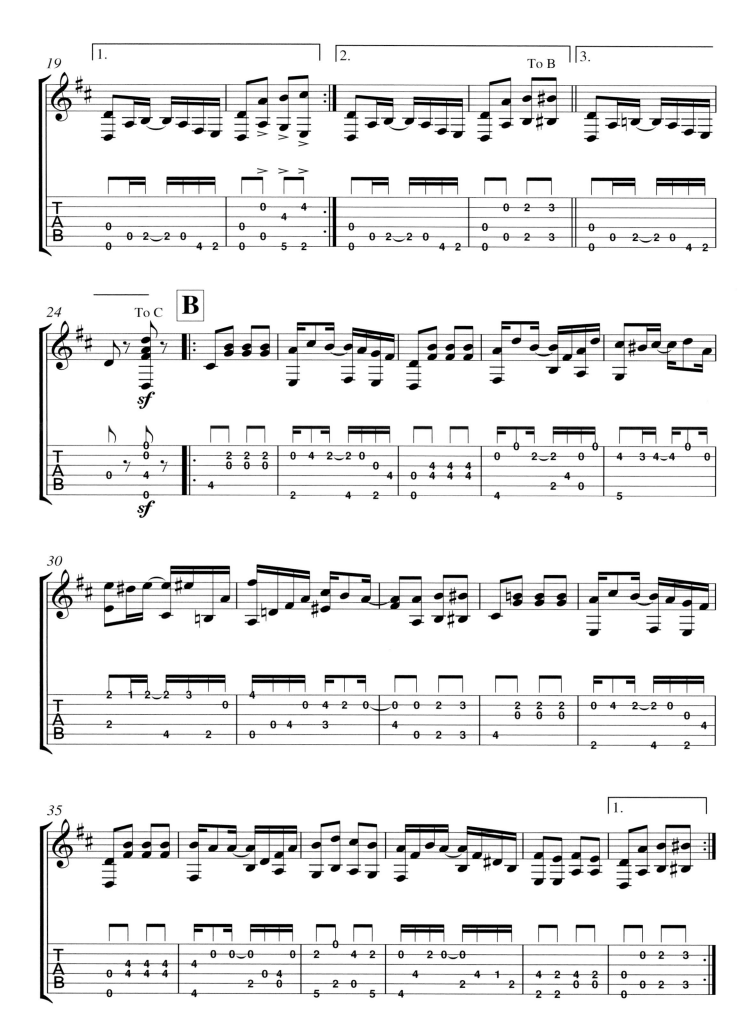

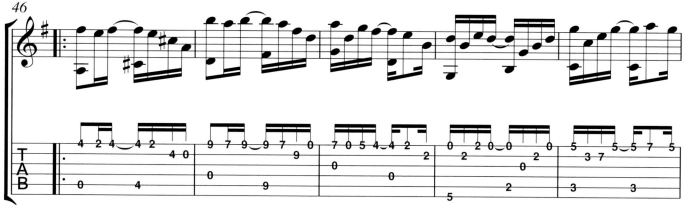

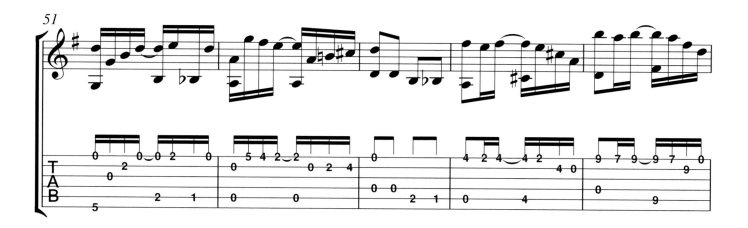

Sunflower Dance

Form: AABACCABA

Arr. Rob MacKillop

Herman Rowland

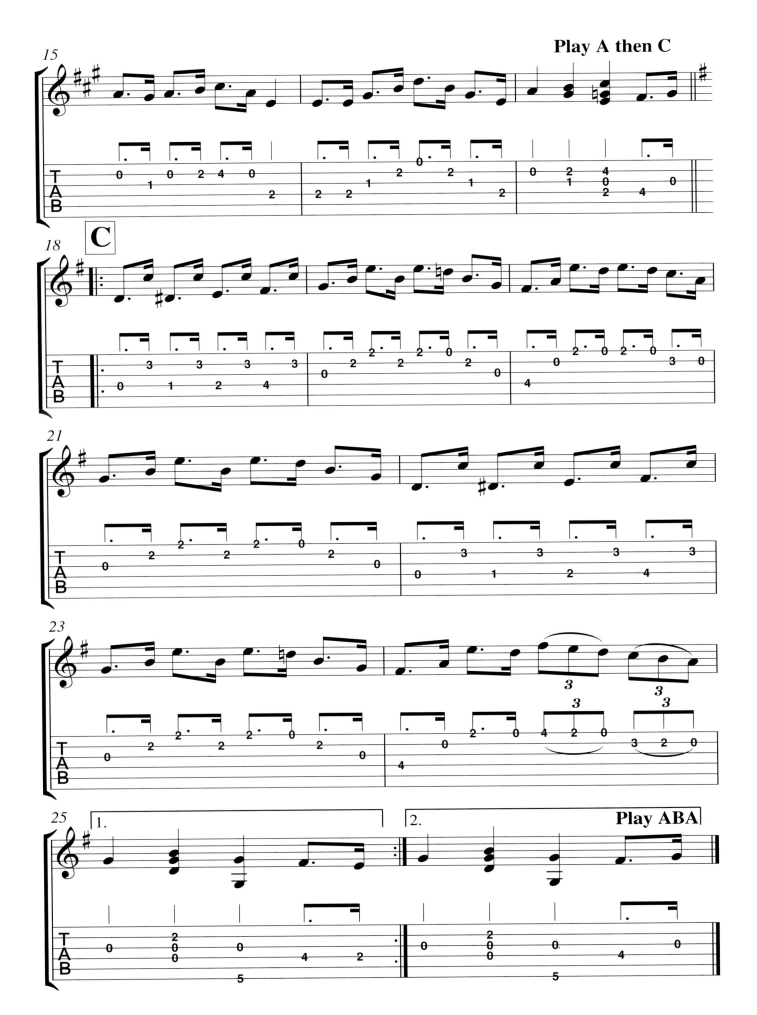

The Entertainer
Form: IntroAABBACCDD

Arranged by
Rob MacKillop

Scott Joplin

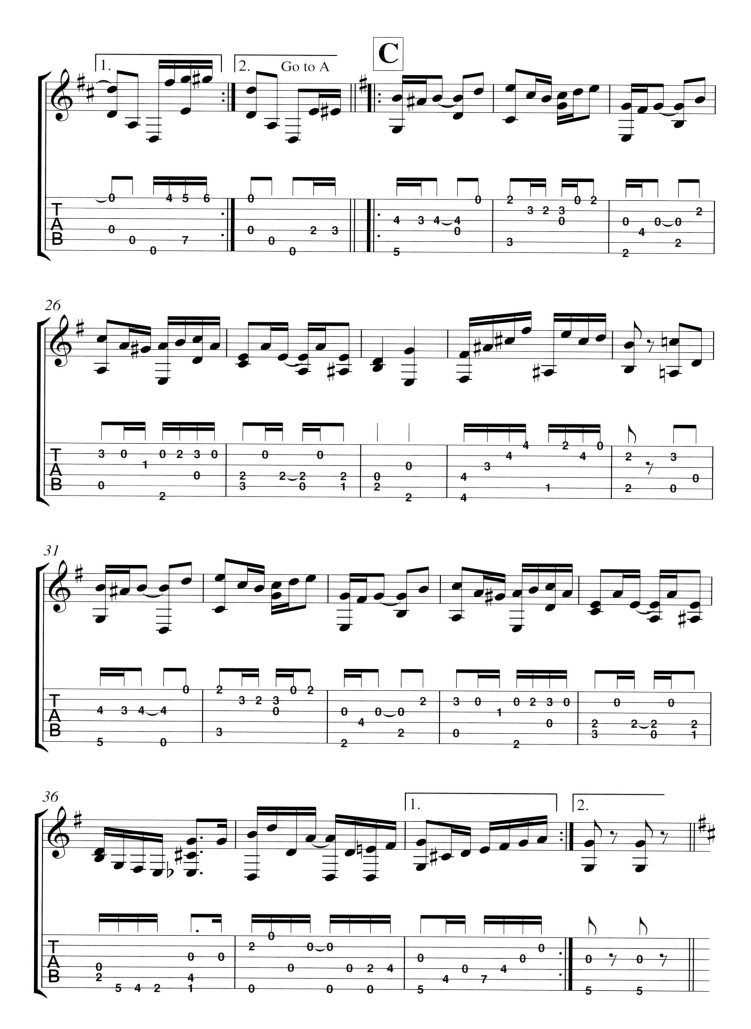

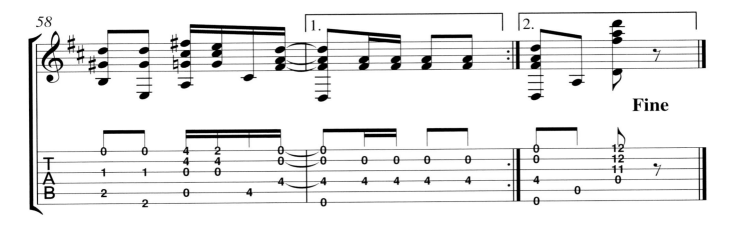

Weeping Willow

Arr. Rob MacKillop

Scott Joplin

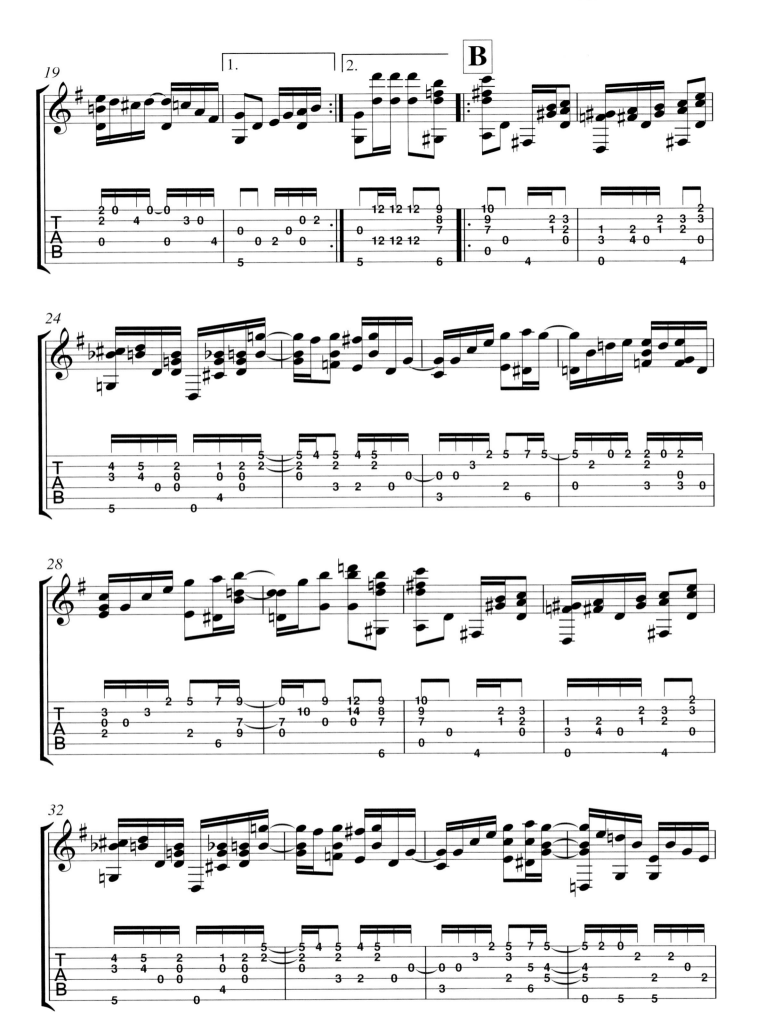

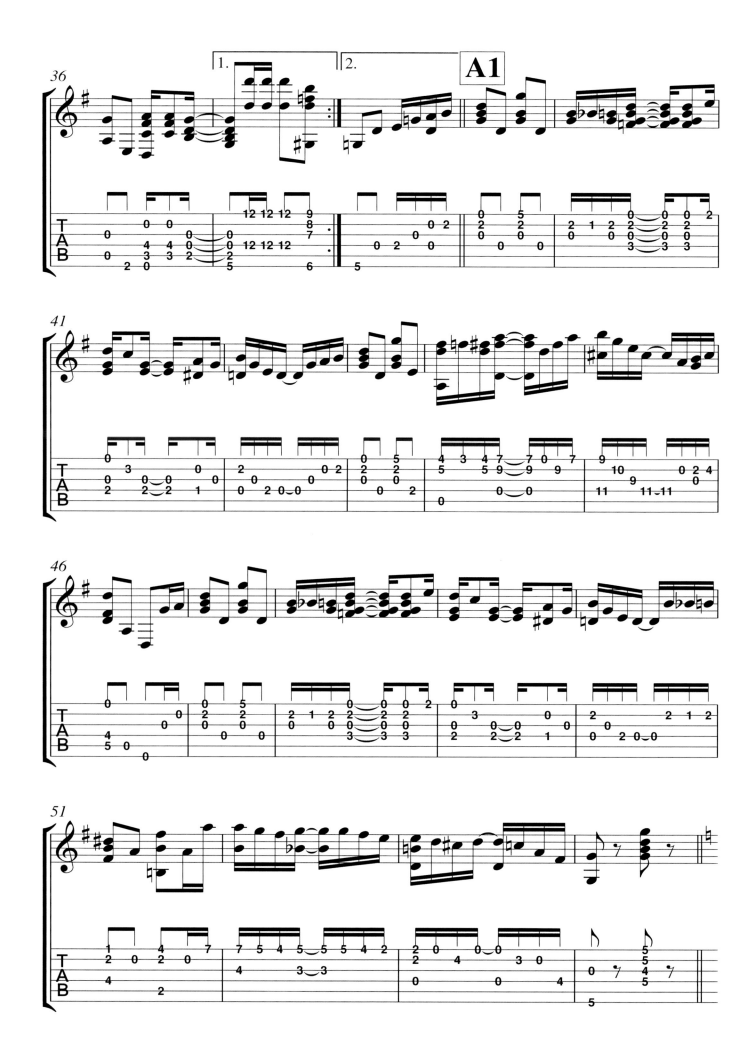

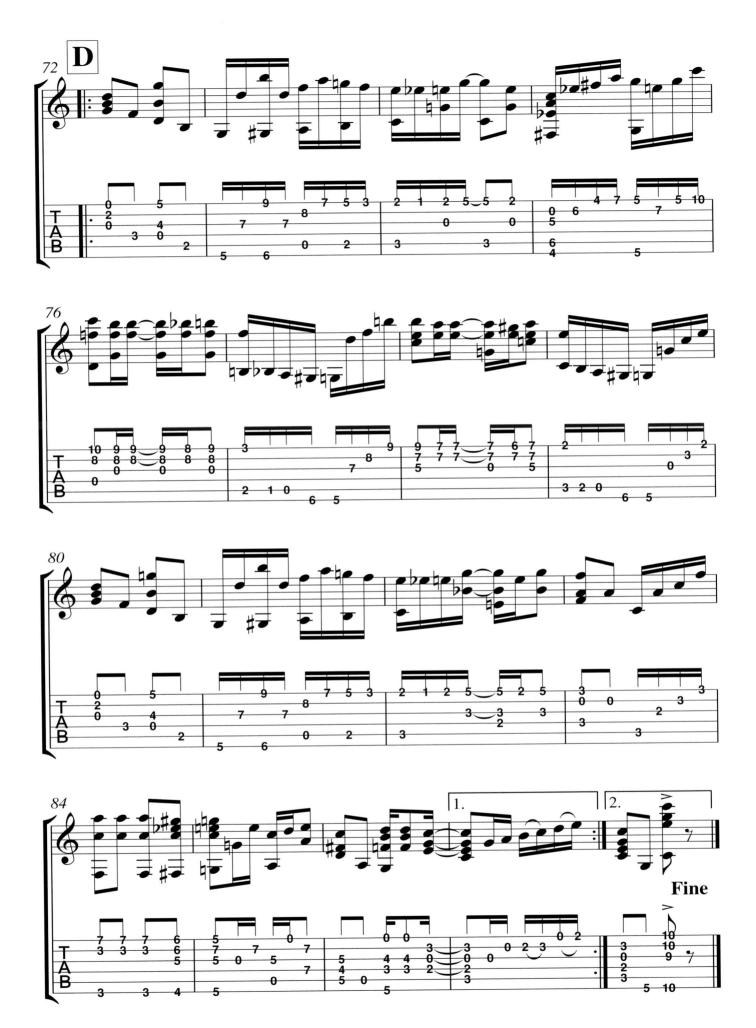

Rob MacKillop

"One of Scotland's finest musicians" *Celtic World*
"A top-drawer player" *Early Music Today*
"MacKillop displays dazzling virtuosity...the playing is exceptionally musical"
Sounding Strings

Rob MacKillop has recorded eight CDs of historical music, three of which reached the Number One position in the Scottish Classical Music Chart. In 2001 he was awarded a Churchill Fellowship for his research into medieval Scottish music, which led him to study with Sufi musicians in Istanbul and Morocco. He broadcast an entire solo concert on BBC Radio 3 from John Smith's Square, London. He has presented academic papers at conferences in Portugal and Germany, and has been published many times. Rob has been active in both historical and contemporary music.

Three of Scotland's leading contemporary composers have written works for him, and he also composes new works himself. In 2004 he was Composer in Residence for Morgan Academy in Dundee, and in 2001 was Musician in Residence for Madras College in St. Andrews. He created and directed the Dundee Summer Music Festival.

He worked as a reader of school literature for Oxford University Press, and as a reviewer for *Music Teacher*. He has also been a lecturer in Scottish Musical History at Aberdeen University, Dundee University, and at the Royal Scottish Academy of Music and Drama, and for five years worked as Musician in Residence to Queen Margaret University in Edinburgh. He has frequently written articles for *BMG Magazine.*

Rob plays guitars, lutes, 18th-century wire-strung "guittar," plucking the strings with the flesh of his fingers, not the nails. This produces a warm and intimate sound, reminiscent of the old lute players.

Rob MacKillop is at the forefront of the revival of historical guitar styles, performing on period and modern instruments. These days he teaches from his home studio in Edinburgh, Scotland, as well as via Skype.

Rob has written many books for Mel Bay Publications.

Other Recommended Books

Easy DADGAD Classics for Acoustic Guitar (MacKillop)

DADGAD Blues (MacKillop)

Easy DADGAD Celtic Guitar (MacKillop)

DADGAD: Old-Time, Flatpicking and Bluegrass (MacKillop)

DADGAD and DGDGCD Tunings (Henigan)

DADGAD Chords, Scales & Tuning (Schell)

Fiddle Tunes in DADGAD (Young)

DADGAD Encyclopedia (Goodin)

DADGAD Tuning (Henigan)

Understanding DADGAD (Young)

Early Jazz for Fingerstyle Guitar (Johansson)

Dixieland Tunes for Fingerstyle Guitar (Flint)

New Orleans Jazz for Fingerstyle Guitar (Hancoff)

Complete Works of Scott Joplin (de Chiaro)

Ragtime Guitar (Grossman)

Classic Ragtime Guitar (Grossman, Baker, Wijnkamp, Jr.)

Blues and Ragtime Fingerstyle Guitar (Van Ronk)

www.melbay.com

WWW.MELBAY.COM